Original title:
Murmurs Beneath Rainlit Trails

Author: Paulina Pähkel
ISBN HARDBACK: 978-9908-1-6019-1
ISBN PAPERBACK: 978-9908-1-6020-7
ISBN EBOOK: 978-9908-1-6021-4

Echoes of the Forgotten Trail

In the soft light of dawn's embrace,
Whispers of silence fill the air.
Footsteps tread on ancient space,
Where memories linger, unaware.

Branches sway with secrets old,
Leaves rustle with stories untold.
In shadows deep, the heart grows bold,
As echoes of the past unfold.

A stream flows gently, clear and bright,
Reflecting tales of those who roamed.
With every ripple, a fleeting sight,
Of wanderers that called this home.

Mountains stand in silent grace,
Guardians of the wanderer's quest.
Their peaks hold time in a warm embrace,
Inviting souls to find their rest.

The trail winds on, a path revealed,
Through fields where wildflowers bloom.
In every turn, the heart is healed,
As nature's voice dispels the gloom.

Enigmas Wrapped in Raindrops

Raindrops fall, secrets spill,
Nature whispers, time stands still.
Mysteries dance on every pane,
Each droplet holds a story's reign.

Hidden dreams drift in the air,
Clouds conceal what we all share.
A puzzle formed in grayish hue,
Unraveled only by the few.

In every plink, a voice unheard,
Fragments lost in softest word.
A tapestry of joy and woe,
Within the rain, emotions flow.

Rainy Day Reveries

Upon the windows, shadows play,
Thoughts wander in the soft decay.
Puddles form in quiet streets,
Where dreamers drift and time retreats.

The gray sky holds a quiet song,
A symphony where we belong.
With tea in hand, we sit and muse,
Reflecting on the paths we choose.

Every raindrop, a fleeting chance,
Inviting hearts to softly dance.
In solitude, the blissful ache,
Of rainy days, our souls awake.

Echoing Footsteps on Soggy Soil

Footsteps crunch on sodden ground,
With every step, lost dreams resound.
Mud embraces worn-out shoes,
As echoes sing in the misty hues.

Nature's breath, a fragrant sigh,
Underneath the heavy sky.
Each stride leads to tales untold,
In the rain, memories unfold.

Soggy paths, where shadows roam,
Each puddle glows like a hidden home.
We wander through the whispered trees,
Carving stories on the breeze.

Gentle Songs from the Gloom

In the heart of the darkened gray,
Gentle songs begin to play.
Softening burdens with every note,
A melody on which we float.

The world slows in a sweet embrace,
While raindrops weave their tender lace.
Cascading lullabies serene,
Soothing whispers in between.

Amidst the gloom, a lantern glows,
Lighting paths where love still flows.
With every chord, the heart finds peace,
In gentle songs, our worries cease.

Whispers on the Wet Path

Footsteps soft, the puddles gleam,
Echoes whisper, lost in dream.
Silent tales, the night unfolds,
Carried secrets, softly told.

Moonlight dances on the street,
Where the rain and shadows meet.
Nature's breath, a tender sigh,
Calling hearts to wander by.

Leaves are glistening, fresh and bright,
Mingling shadows with the light.
Every drop a sweet refrain,
Telling stories of the rain.

Footfalls gentle, travelers roam,
In the silence, they find home.
Gentle echoes linger near,
Whispers soft for those who hear.

Through the night, the path will weave,
In each corner, hearts believe.
Guided by the rain's embrace,
Finding warmth in every place.

Secrets of the Soaked Earth

Beneath the soil, the stories lie,
Tales of old, where roots apply.
Secrets whispered through the rain,
Nurtured deep in quiet pain.

The flowers bloom, in color bright,
Drinking deep of nature's light.
Earth embraces all it knows,
In the depths, wisdom grows.

Raindrops drip on leaves so green,
Painting glories yet unseen.
Rivers swell with tales to tell,
In the silence, we can dwell.

Molded shapes, in clay we find,
Echoes of the ancient kind.
Nature holds its breath in trust,
Yearning hearts return to dust.

The forest speaks, in rustle low,
Secrets shared in ebb and flow.
Traces of the past remain,
Whisper softly through the rain.

Echoes in the Pattering Night

Night unfolds with gentle shower,
Sounds of life in nature's power.
Pattering soft on window panes,
Echoing the world's sweet strains.

In the stillness, music plays,
Rhythms pulse in secret ways.
Every note, a story spun,
Crafted under moonlit run.

Hearts awaken, dreams take flight,
Lost in echoes, wrapped in night.
Whispers dance on soft night air,
Carried forth from everywhere.

Through the dark, the symphony,
Guides the soul to harmony.
Pattering songs, the raindrops sing,
Nature's voice, a sacred ring.

In the quiet, spirits soar,
With each beat, we seek for more.
Echoes of a fleeting time,
Resonate in rhythmic rhyme.

Shadows Beneath Silver Skies

Silver hues in twilight glow,
Casting shadows soft and slow.
Underneath the canopy,
Mysterious lives wait to see.

Gentle breezes through the leaves,
Whisper secrets as one weaves.
Dance of light, a fleeting trace,
In the shadows, we find grace.

Nighttime calls in hushed delight,
Softly wrapping all in night.
Moonbeams spark on water's face,
Creating magic, time's embrace.

Every rustle, every sigh,
Echoes of the night go by.
Underneath the silver skies,
Nature breathes, and softly lies.

In the quiet, dreams take flight,
Drawing shadows into light.
A tapestry of dark and bright,
Unfolds beneath the starlit night.

Cadence of the Cascading Drops

Droplets dance on leaves so green,
Whispers soft, a gentle queen.
Nature's symphony does play,
In hues of gold and silver gray.

Echoes splash in perfect time,
Beating hearts, a fleeting rhyme.
Silver threads on the ground weave,
A tapestry for all to grieve.

Over rocks, the waters flow,
Secrets carved in ebb and glow.
Every drop a story told,
In whispers soft, life's truths unfold.

Clouds embrace the earth's sweet breath,
Painting shadows that dance with death.
Yet through gloom, a light does shine,
In every drop, a hope divine.

Listen close, to nature's song,
Feel the pulse where you belong.
In the cadence, find your peace,
In each drop, let worries cease.

Musings in a Misty Veil

Morning breaks with gentle sighs,
Misty veils in muted highs.
Silhouettes in soft embrace,
Nature's art, a quiet grace.

Whispers wrap the world in dreams,
Flowing forward, hidden streams.
Each breath stirs the hazy air,
Thoughts alight, free from care.

Footsteps trace the paths unknown,
In the fog, seeds of thoughts are sown.
Echoes fade in twilight's glow,
Where the mind is free to flow.

Patterns swirl in the morning mist,
Moments caught, impossible to resist.
Tales of wonder yet to be,
In each droplet, life's mystery.

Underneath this veil of gray,
Beauty hides in disarray.
Softly now, embrace the chill,
Let your heart learn to be still.

Rhythm of the Rain-Kissed Trail

Footprints on the wet, cool ground,
Nature's music sings around.
Rhythms of the softest rain,
A delicate, sweet refrain.

Leaves shimmer in the morning light,
A canvas painted, pure delight.
Each step echoes, pulse alive,
In the rhythm, hearts will thrive.

Puddles form like little dreams,
Reflecting world in shifting seems.
Every splash a fleeting glee,
In the dance, just let it be.

Gentle breezes weave through trees,
Rustles whisper, secrets tease.
Guided by the water's song,
In this rhythm, we belong.

With each drop, the story grows,
In the trail, where nature flows.
Let the rain wash cares away,
Join the dance, come what may.

Intimacies of the Glistening Ground

After rain, the earth does gleam,
Reflecting life, a waking dream.
In the hush, soft whispers blend,
Nature's call, our hearts ascend.

Stones and soil, a secret pact,
Every drop a precious act.
Glistening tales beneath our feet,
In the mud, where worlds do meet.

Dewdrops cling like little gems,
Nature's sweet and tender hems.
Kissed by sun and kissed by rain,
In this beauty, we remain.

Every shadow tells a tale,
Of storms endured and love's unveil.
In the rhythm of the ground,
Life's intimacy is found.

Winds will sing and birds will call,
In this space, we feel it all.
Join the earth in dance so true,
Glistening ground, we shine with you.

The Sound of Journeying Streams

Soft whispers flow down the hill,
Gentle songs from waters still.
They carve their path through ancient stone,
A melody of nature's own.

Sunlight dances on the wave,
Each ripple tells of earth so brave.
With every twist, each turn and bend,
The stream unravels, journeys blend.

Birds above in chorus sing,
As currents swirl, their voices cling.
Reflections shimmer, crystal clear,
The journey calls, the trails appear.

Along the bank, the wildflowers sway,
In harmony with the stream's ballet.
A tale of time, forever told,
In sounds of life, both new and old.

Echoes linger, as day grows dim,
The twilight hum, a haunting hymn.
In every drop, a secret gleams,
The sound of life, of journeying streams.

Voices Hidden in Glistening Shadows

Beneath the trees, where daylight fades,
Whispers float in soft cascades.
Glistening hues paint silent dreams,
Voices linger in twilight beams.

Shadows stretch, embracing night,
Crafting tales in fading light.
Secrets spun in silver threads,
Softly spoken, as daylight sheds.

Echoes shimmer on the breeze,
Carried forth through rustling leaves.
Their melody a gentle sigh,
Hidden truths that softly pry.

Glimmers spark in quiet guise,
As stars awaken in the skies.
Softly calling, the night grows near,
Voices hidden soon appear.

Within the dusk, where shadows play,
Mysteries weave, drifting away.
In every whisper, life flows on,
The hidden voices of the dawn.

Rustling Leaves and Raindrop Reveries

In gentle falls, the raindrops sing,
Rustling leaves in joy take wing.
Each pitter-patter tells a tale,
Of nature's heart in rhythmic wail.

Underneath a silver sky,
The world awakes, the dreamers sigh.
Whispers of the earth's sweet breath,
In every drop, a dance with death.

The forest hums in harmony,
A tranquil choir, wild and free.
Raindrop reveries, soft and sweet,
In every beat, a heartbeat's greet.

Leaves embrace the beauty poured,
A symphony without a chord.
As puddles form, reflections spin,
The dance of dreams, an endless win.

Every rustle, every sound,
A moment's peace is always found.
In nature's song, we find our way,
Rustling leaves and raindrop play.

Beneath the Canopy's Gentle Cry

Underneath the canopy's fold,
Stories of the forest told.
Gentle cries in whispers seep,
Awakening the woods from sleep.

Mossy paths in sunlight gleam,
Nature's embrace, a waking dream.
In muted hues, life finds a way,
Beneath the boughs, night greets the day.

Softly sighing, the branches sway,
A lullaby that will not stray.
The echoes dance in twilight's show,
As stars arrive, the shadows glow.

Creatures stir, their secrets shared,
Stories told of those who dared.
In every leaf, a pulse, a sigh,
Beneath the canopy's gentle cry.

Through the ages, time will weave,
A tapestry of those who believe.
In silent moments, truth is found,
Under boughs where love is crowned.

Laughter in the Puddled Reflections

Children leap with carefree glee,
Shadows dance in puddled cheer.
Raindrops mimic their laughter,
Nature joins in the bright flair.

Ripples send soft whispers round,
Mirrored smiles in every face.
Joy erupts from the ground,
As droplets drink the sun's grace.

Colors shimmer in splashed delight,
Every heartbeat stirs the mud.
They twirl in a world of bright,
Where laughter flows like a flood.

Winds carry a sweet refrain,
As the clouds begin to part.
Sunlight plays its gentle game,
Imprinting warmth within the heart.

In each splash, a memory made,
Of childhood's thrilling embrace.
Puddles born from rain's cascade,
Hold joy in their tender trace.

The Language of Stormy Breezes

Whispers rise in violent air,
Tales of thunder, lightning's fire.
Breezes carry secrets rare,
Of nature's wild and fierce desire.

Trees sway gently, bend like grass,
Roots in prayer, strong and deep.
Stormy winds like spirits pass,
Awakening dreams from sleep.

Clouds speak in a rumbling voice,
Channeling thunder's mighty scream.
Winds compel the heart to rejoice,
Lauding life's tempestuous dream.

Each gust paints the sky with lore,
Eager to share the tempest's might.
In the storm, our spirits soar,
As whispers dance in the twilight.

Their rhythms pulse with ancient grace,
In every breeze, a story twined.
Nature's language, fierce embrace,
In storm, our hearts are refined.

Serenade of the Sopping Stones

Wet stones sing in sighs of rain,
Every drop a note, a sound.
Nature's hymn, a soft refrain,
Where the water's art is found.

Mossy cloaks on ancient beds,
Whispers of the stream flow free.
Each stone cradles tales itd read,
History carved in time's decree.

Streams weave lightly through the glade,
Mirroring the night's sweet tune.
Underneath the leafy shade,
Nature dances 'neath the moon.

Serenity in water's grace,
Every pebble plays its part.
Harmony found in this place,
Echoes spoken from the heart.

In quiet cadence, thoughts roam wide,
The serenade of soaked embrace.
In every droplet, dreams reside,
Holding whispers time can't erase.

Trails of Teardrop Trails

Each teardrop finds its way to earth,
Paths of sorrow softly tread.
In their wake, a silent mirth,
Healing light where pain once led.

Through the gloom, they carve a line,
Sketching stories, faint yet clear.
From the heart, a voice divine,
Echoes of love, deep and near.

Footprints marked by loss and grace,
Every drop, a step to take.
In their flow, they trace the space,
Where the heart begins to wake.

Through the storm, our spirits climb,
Teardrops fall as nature wills.
In each we find the thread of time,
Binding joy in heartbeats still.

From sadness blooms a gentle peace,
A trail where hope can freely grow.
With every drop, our worries cease,
In teardrop trails, love's light will glow.

Tides of Emotion on Rainy Roads

The raindrops dance on asphalt bright,
Reflecting dreams in silver light.
Wheels whisper secrets, quiet and low,
As feelings ebb and flow, they glow.

Puddles form like tears in time,
Each ripple carries a silent rhyme.
Fog embraces the fading sun,
In this storm, all hearts are one.

Emotions rise with every wave,
A tempest wild, yet souls are brave.
Lost in thought, we drift and sway,
On rainy roads, we find our way.

The night descends, the skies now dark,
Stormy skies ignite a spark.
With every turn, the shadows play,
In tides of emotion, we find our way.

Through fleeting moments, we let go,
Together here, in rain's soft flow.
Bound by whispers, we journey on,
In the dance of the tides, we are drawn.

Beneath the Clouds Shedding Memories

Beneath the clouds, where dreams reside,
We find the whispers long denied.
Each droplet bears a lost refrain,
A symphony of joy and pain.

The grey above begins to spill,
Each memory held, a gentle thrill.
Faces seen through misty eyes,
Beneath the clouds, no need for lies.

Faded laughter, echoes near,
With every drop, we shed a tear.
In these moments, we reclaim,
Beneath the clouds, we all feel the same.

Past and present intertwine,
In the rain, the edges blur, align.
Fragments scattered, lost but brave,
Under the clouds, together we crave.

Embers flicker, hearts ignite,
New memories formed in the night.
In rain's embrace, we find our peace,
Beneath the clouds, our worries cease.

Echoes Carried by the November Fog

In November's chill, the fog rolls deep,
Carrying echoes, secrets to keep.
Ghostly whispers through the trees,
Memories sway with the autumn breeze.

Footsteps muffled, thoughts entwined,
In the haze, solace we find.
Each breath a mist, each sigh a song,
In the fog, we feel we belong.

Winding paths lead us astray,
Yet in this stillness, we choose to stay.
Voices linger, soft and low,
Carried forth in the November glow.

Reflections surface, lost in time,
In the quiet, hearts begin to chime.
As daylight fades, our spirits soar,
Echoes carried, forever more.

Through the shroud, we dance and weave,
In the embrace of what we believe.
Hidden truths begin to show,
In echoes carried by the fog's soft flow.

Silent Stories Between Each Drop

Each drop a whisper, soft and clear,
Tales of longing, hearts draw near.
In the silence, stories unfold,
Between each drop, a moment told.

Pattering rhythms, nature's song,
In the stillness, where we belong.
Through life's canvas, colors bleed,
Between each drop, our souls are freed.

The world slows down, breath held tight,
As raindrops dance in fragile light.
Caught in the magic, we become,
Silent stories, without a drum.

Memories drip like dew on grass,
In this moment, we let them pass.
With each fall, we learn and grow,
Silent stories, the rain's soft glow.

In every tear shed, every cheer,
Between each drop, love draws near.
Together we share, together we keep,
The silent stories that make us weep.

Pathways Drizzled with Dreams

On golden paths where shadows play,
Whispers dance in twilight's sway.
Moments caught like fleeting streams,
Life unfolds in secret dreams.

Beneath the arch of azure skies,
Hope takes flight, its wings arise.
With every step, the heart believes,
In the magic that never leaves.

Flowers bloom in gentle sighs,
Coloring all in soft goodbyes.
Silver threads of starlit lore,
Guide us to what we seek and more.

Through forests deep and valleys wide,
We wander with our hearts as guide.
Each turn reveals a hidden theme,
In pathways drizzled with dreams.

In the dusk, the silence hums,
Echoes of a world that comes.
Every corner, a story gleams,
In the fabric of our dreams.

Echoed Laments of a Rainy Embrace

Softly falling, silver tears,
Kiss the earth, calm our fears.
In their rhythm, heartbeats find,
Echoes linger, intertwined.

Clouds gather, a somber cloak,
Within the hush, the raindrops spoke.
Each droplet carries silent cries,
In the landscape where love lies.

Puddles form, reflecting sighs,
Mirrored dreams of distant skies.
In the dance of stormy grace,
We find solace in this space.

Umbrellas bloom like flowers bright,
Shielding lovers in the night.
In the downpour, hearts embrace,
Echoed laments in a warm place.

Fingers trace the sultry air,
Holding tight to whispered prayers.
Through the gloom, we twine and roam,
In the rain, we find a home.

Secrets From a Weeping Sky

Above, the heavens softly weep,
Moisture drips while moments seep.
Every cloud a tale untold,
Secrets hidden, bright yet cold.

As shadows fall, the dusk reveals,
Whispers wrapped in silver peels.
The world beneath, drenched in sighs,
Listens close to the weeping skies.

Starlight flickers far away,
Guiding hopes in muted gray.
Nature's tears form rivers wide,
Washing dreams we cannot hide.

In the quiet, hearts confess,
Longing wrapped in crazed finesse.
From the sky, we sense the hand,
Of fate's brush, both stern and grand.

Secrets shared, a longing sigh,
Underneath this weeping sky.
In the droplets, stories blend,
Temporal whispers that transcend.

Songs of the Grey Horizon

In twilight's glow, the world aligns,
A canvas brushed with crossed designs.
Soft echoes spill like gentle rain,
Songs arise from joy and pain.

Each note carries a tale of old,
In woven chords, the heart is bold.
Underneath the muted light,
Dreams take flight, both day and night.

Air is thick with promises made,
In every shadow, sunlight fade.
Harmony in life's embrace,
Songs of hope, we find our place.

With dawn's retreat and dusk's accord,
The Grey Horizon sings once more.
In whispers soft, we find our way,
Chasing colors as we sway.

To the rhythm of time's gentle roll,
We dance along to nature's soul.
In this journey, we belong,
Forever lost in the song.

Threads of Life Through the Rain's Embrace

Pattering drops on the ground,
Whispering tales all around.
Each splash a life, a story spun,
In the dance of rain, we run.

Nature's quilt, a vibrant weave,
Carried dreams on a breeze.
Threads of life, woven tight,
In every storm, there's a light.

Clouds gather, dark and low,
Yet beneath, the flowers grow.
Roots dig deeper in the clay,
Chasing hope in a gentle sway.

With each drop, fears dissolve,
In the mud, we choose to evolve.
Embrace the tears, let them flow,
For in the rain, our spirits glow.

So let us tread this winding path,
Find joy in storms, escape the wrath.
Threads of life, forever binding,
In the rain's embrace, love is finding.

Dreams etching Loamy Soil

In fields where whispers play,
Seeds of hope find their way.
Dreams take root in loamy beds,
Nurtured by words left unsaid.

Each sprout a wish, a gentle sigh,
Reaching upward toward the sky.
Beneath the earth, a hidden quest,
Life unfolds, unconfessed.

Fingers in dirt, we cultivate,
Planting dreams, we celebrate.
Nature's canvas, rich and bold,
Stories of life, silently told.

Sunrise hues paint the dawn,
With every ray, the night is gone.
In the soil, our heartbeats dwell,
Each seed sown, a wish to tell.

As seasons change, we watch and learn,
From every growing twist and turn.
Dreams take flight, and souls arise,
In loamy soil, we touch the skies.

The Gentle Roar of Hidden Streams

In valleys deep, where shadows lie,
Soft waters hum, a lullaby.
Hidden streams weave through the trees,
Their gentle roar whispers with ease.

Crystals dance on rocky beds,
While sunlight flickers, softly spreads.
In the glen, where silence reigns,
The heart finds peace, and joy remains.

Winding paths of whispered grace,
Nature's pulse, a soft embrace.
Flowing echoes through lush green,
In hidden depths, beauty's seen.

Beneath the surface, life abounds,
In every ripple, wonder sounds.
As waters course through time's embrace,
The hidden streams reveal their place.

So listen close to gentle flow,
The stories that the waters know.
In each ripple, wisdom gleams,
The gentle roar of hidden streams.

Secrets Revealed by Autumn's Tears

Leaves of gold drift down like dreams,
Carpeting earth with muted schemes.
In the crisp air, secrets sigh,
As autumn whispers goodbye.

Every breeze carries a tale,
Of summer's warmth, of winter's pale.
Secrets churn in shades of red,
In every falling leaf, they spread.

Pine trees stand, steadfast and true,
While shadows stretch, as twilight grew.
Nature's canvas, changes reveal,
In the silence, what we feel.

Candles flicker, nights grow long,
In cozy nooks, we find our song.
Embrace the chill, let shadows reign,
For autumn's tears wash away the pain.

With every gust, we let go fears,
Gathering strength through autumn's tears.
In the hush, we rediscover,
Secrets kept by each lost lover.

Serenity in a Shower's Embrace

Raindrops gently kiss my face,
Each one a soft, sweet grace.
The world slows beneath the grey,
In silence where my thoughts can play.

Clouds wrap me in their embrace,
A soothing balm, a tender space.
Each droplet sings of peace and calm,
A nature's gift, a soothing balm.

Footsteps dance in puddles near,
Each splash a song, so crystal clear.
In these moments, I am free,
Inspired by the symphony of glee.

The air is fresh, the heart is light,
In this shower, I find delight.
With every drop, my soul's set free,
In the embrace of rain's decree.

Life's worries wash away with ease,
In twilight's glow, I find my peace.
As skies weep and spirits soar,
I cherish this, forever more.

Echoing Heartbeats of the Falling Sky

The thunder rolls, a mighty roar,
Nature's heartbeat, forevermore.
Each droplet whispers tales untold,
In the arms of storm, I feel bold.

Lightning flickers, bright and wild,
In the tempest, I become a child.
With every crash, I find my place,
A canvas painted with wild grace.

Clouds hang heavy, a tattered cloak,
Hiding secrets that they spoke.
As rain begins to kiss the ground,
Every heartbeat, a softer sound.

In this dance of dark and light,
Fear and beauty become one flight.
With open arms, the world does sigh,
Echoing heartbeats of the falling sky.

Nature's pulse in rhythmic flow,
A bond unbroken, fierce yet slow.
With every storm, I learn to fly,
In the echoes of the swaying sky.

Whispers in the Puddles

Mirrored skies in puddles lie,
Captured dreams that float and sigh.
Each ripple tells a story clear,
Of moments held, both far and near.

Children dance and laughter swirls,
In reflections, their joy unfurls.
Tiny worlds beneath the rain,
Whispers soft, a sweet refrain.

Clouds drift low, a blanket grey,
As whispers guide the wandering way.
In every splash, a secret shared,
Nature's voice shows that it cared.

Footsteps soft on muddy ground,
In puddles' depths, new dreams are found.
Life in droplets, bright and bold,
A tapestry of stories told.

With every glance, futures align,
In puddles' depths, fragments shine.
Whispers linger, soft and sweet,
In this dance, my heart finds beat.

Secrets of the Silvered Path

A winding trail of glistening light,
Silvered paths in the moon's delight.
Each step a secret, soft and sly,
Calling forth dreams as shadows fly.

Whispers float on the midnight air,
Tales of old that spark a dare.
In the silence, truths unveil,
On this path where spirits sail.

The silver glow guides my way,
Through the night and into day.
With every breath, I feel the pull,
Of mysteries that make me full.

Nature hums a sacred tune,
Underneath the watching moon.
In the shadows, visions gleam,
As heartbeats weave their gentle dream.

In each footstep, paths converge,
As nature sings, my spirit surge.
Secrets whispered in the dark,
Light the way and leave a mark.

Dance of the Water-Whipped Breeze

Whispers of the river flow,
Softly in the twilight glow.
The grasses sway, a gentle tease,
Nature sings with water-whipped breeze.

Moonlight glimmers on the stream,
Stars reflect in silver dream.
A symphony of nights embrace,
Dancing shadows find their place.

Ripples chase the fading light,
Breath of evening, soft and bright.
Each turn tells an ancient tale,
Where echoes of the wild prevail.

In the hush, the spirit plays,
Life awakens in a daze.
The world holds its breath, stands still,
Enchanted by the water's thrill.

Let us join this wild ballet,
Hearts entwined in night's soft sway.
As nature leads with gentle hand,
We find our joy in wonderland.

Hushed Exchanges Along the Soggy Trail

Footsteps echo, soft and low,
Moisture lingers, earth's shadow.
Ferns nod gently, whispers glide,
Secrets shared where dreams abide.

The path winds through the ancient trees,
Crickets chirp with each soft breeze.
Raindrops nestle, a tender kiss,
In this world, we find our bliss.

Misty corners, thoughts entwined,
Nature's calm, our spirits lined.
In the hush, we pause to hear,
All the stories drawing near.

Every puddle holds a face,
Reflections caught in soulful grace.
A dance of moments, both shy and bold,
Here in silence, love unfolds.

With each step, a tale retold,
Nature's warmth, a hand to hold.
In the quiet, hearts will sail,
Hushed exchanges on the trail.

Shades of Memory in Raindrop Rivulets

Raindrops trace on window panes,
Softly carving out our pains.
Shades of memory, grey and blue,
Whisper tales of me and you.

Each drop a moment, washed away,
Yet in their fall, we find our way.
Fragments echo in the rain,
Songs of joy, and hints of pain.

A puddle holds a laughter's sound,
In the stillness, love is found.
Mirrored paths of past embrace,
Raindrop rivulets softly trace.

Tender stories gently flow,
In the droplets, hearts aglow.
Each memory a fleeting spark,
Lighting shadows, breaking dark.

As clouds recede, the world awakes,
In each rivulet, a chance to take.
Shades of memory, time does weave,
In every raindrop, we believe.

Forgotten Stories Under Silvered Skies

Beneath the stars, the night holds sway,
Whispered legends drift away.
In the dark, the tales unfold,
Forgotten dreams, now spoken bold.

Silvered skies with stories drawn,
A tapestry of dusk till dawn.
Voices weaving through the air,
Ancient echoes, sweet and rare.

Flickering lights, a gentle tease,
Memories dance with playful ease.
In every shadow, myths reside,
Waiting for the heart to guide.

Lost histories in velvet night,
Wisdom glimmers, purest light.
In the calm, the truth may rise,
Forgotten stories, timeless ties.

So let us listen, hearts awake,
Every sigh, each choice we make.
Under silvered skies, we find,
The treasure hidden in the mind.

Tales Carried by Soft Drizzles

Whispers weave through the air,
Gentle stories beg to be heard.
Each drop a tale of the sky,
Dancing lightly on the ground.

Moonlight fades with the dusk,
Raindrops kiss the thirsty earth.
Laughter echoes in soft tones,
Nature breathes in sweet relief.

Silken threads of silver fall,
Embracing flowers, trees, and stone.
In their rhythm, peace is found,
In their hush, the world slows down.

Softly rustling leaves at night,
The drizzles play a lullaby.
Every leaf holds droplets tight,
Guarding tales from days gone by.

With each sigh, the leaves reply,
In their hold, dreams begin to swell.
Carried forth, they softly fly,
Tales of hope in every swell.

The Quiet Song of Fallen Drops

Fallen drops in twilight's glow,
Sing of secrets, soft and low.
They gather round the old stone path,
In silence, crafting nature's math.

Rippling echoes through the air,
Each drop sings without a care.
Joining in a gentle tune,
Murmured by the silver moon.

With every touch of misty night,
A canvas drawn in purest light.
Songs of whispers fill the air,
Notes of love without a care.

Through the darkness, voices blend,
A soft hymn that will not end.
In their chorus, dreams arise,
Painting tales across the skies.

Lost in magic, hush prevails,
Each drop a note that never fails.
The quiet song gently flows,
In the heart, its rhythm grows.

Dreams Drift on Drenched Floors

On the floor, the dreams do flow,
Dancing softly, twirling slow.
Puddles mirror the sky's embrace,
A world renewed in a gentle space.

Raindrops weave through memories bright,
Whispers of the day and night.
Beneath the clouds, colors blend,
As shadows stretch and softly mend.

In the corners, silence rests,
Threads of peace caress our quests.
Time dissolves on this wet ground,
In stillness, beauty's always found.

Each droplet holds a wish on high,
Reflections kiss the wanderer's eye.
Lost hopes and dreams drift away,
On drenched floors where hearts can stay.

With each soft sigh from the trees,
Laughter mingles with the breeze.
Eternal moments start to soar,
As dreams drift softly to the floor.

Lullabies of the Weeping Woods

In weeping woods where secrets sigh,
Lullabies drift, softly nigh.
Branches sway with a gentle grace,
Embracing sorrow, time, and space.

Each raindrop from the boughs above,
Carries whispers of lost love.
Their rhythm sways with evening's light,
Melodies born from fading night.

A symphony of silent cries,
In every drop, a world complies.
The woods weep for forgotten days,
In tender tunes, lost in a haze.

Beneath the canopy so deep,
Nature hums while the earth does weep.
Crickets join the serenade,
In shadows where the past is laid.

As twilight drapes the forest green,
Soft embrace, a calming sheen.
The lullabies of weeping woods,
Offer solace, as nature broods.

Hints of Magic in Raindrops

In the hush of a rainy day,
Whispers dance on puddled clay.
Each droplet holds a light within,
Secrets of where the dreams begin.

Shimmering sparks in gloomy grey,
Nature's brush, a soft ballet.
With every fall, a story's spun,
A tale of magic, just begun.

Listen close to the falling sound,
A heartbeat from the underground.
The world awakes with every drip,
A gentle sigh, a tender slip.

Clouds weave tales in muted grace,
Painting love on nature's face.
Hints of dreams come alive anew,
In every drop, a glimpse of you.

Voices of the Soggy Footprints

In the mud where shadows play,
Footprints linger, then fade away.
Each step whispers stories told,
Of daring hearts and spirits bold.

The ground is soft, the path unclear,
Echoes linger, close and near.
In the silence, find the sounds,
Of hidden joys that life surrounds.

Puddles mirror the skies above,
Reflecting dreams, a tale of love.
The soggy footprints bear the proof,
Of precious moments, quiet truth.

Voices call from the drizzling rain,
Reminding us of joy and pain.
In every step, a memory flows,
In soggy footprints, grandeur grows.

Lullabies of the Falling Sky

As the sun dips, day turns night,
The clouds awake, a soothing sight.
From heavens high, soft tunes arise,
Lullabies drift through starlit skies.

Each little raindrop sings along,
A tender rhythm, nature's song.
The world beneath starts to glow,
In harmony, a gentle flow.

Whispers merge with the evening breeze,
A cosmic dance among the trees.
Stars twinkle, clad in silver light,
While dreams take wing in the soft night.

Lullabies weave a tapestry,
Embracing all in serenity.
As the moon cradles the earth tight,
Stories linger in the night.

Soft Footfalls in the Mist

Through the fog, a quiet grace,
Footfalls trace an unseen place.
Each step whispers, barely heard,
Lost in thoughts, like fallen birds.

Shadows dance in the silver haze,
A world reborn in dreamy ways.
Nature wraps its arms around,
In soft footfalls, peace is found.

Moments fold into the mist,
Like fleeting dreams that can't be kissed.
In the quiet, hearts align,
With every step, we redefine.

A path unknown beneath the shroud,
Where secrets live, whispered loud.
In soft footfalls, we explore,
The beauty of what lies in store.

Echoes Under the Drizzle

Soft whispers ride the breeze,
Raindrops dance on thirsty ground.
Echoes ripple through the trees,
Nature's song in beauty found.

Clouds embrace the fading light,
Shadows linger, softly fall.
In the quiet, hearts feel right,
Harmony begins to call.

Broken paths of shimmering gray,
Lead us where the lost souls meet.
In the drizzle, we shall stay,
Finding solace, pure and sweet.

Footsteps dampened by the rain,
Murmurs blend with evening's sigh.
Through the mist, we let go pain,
As echoes fade, we rise high.

With every drop, a story breathes,
Whispers weaving dreams anew.
Underneath the swaying leaves,
Life is vibrant, fresh with dew.

Shadows on the Glistening Way

As twilight drapes the glowing street,
Shadows stretch and gently sway.
Footsteps echo, soft and fleet,
Guiding hearts upon their way.

Beneath the shimmer, hopes arise,
Every step a tale to tell.
In the night, where silence lies,
Magic wraps us in its spell.

Streetlamps cast a golden hue,
Illuminating paths we take.
In the dark, the world feels new,
Each shadow, a dance we make.

Dreams emerge in gleaming light,
Every glance ignites the soul.
In the silence of the night,
We become the stories whole.

With every twist, the journey flows,
Glistening way whispers of fate.
Through this maze the heart now knows,
Hope and love forever wait.

Reverberations Through Wet Leaves

Rustling whispers fill the air,
Nature's voice in vibrant green.
Life is dancing everywhere,
In the drizzle, calm is seen.

Echoes bounce from branch to ground,
In the forest's tender hold.
Every droplet, every sound,
Tells a story, brave and bold.

Through the trees, a melody,
Soothing rhythms flow and blend.
Each moment's sweet symphony,
Nature's pulse that will not end.

Winding pathways lost in thought,
Shadows flicker, light retreats.
In the quiet, wisdom's sought,
Footsteps softly, time repeats.

As the rain begins to cease,
Leaves awaken, fresh and bright.
In this place, we find our peace,
Reverberations of the night.

Serenity on a Drenched Journey

Winding roads through drizzled skies,
A gentle rhythm, hearts align.
In the rain, our spirit flies,
Finding solace in the time.

Puddles mirror dreams untold,
Each reflection, life's embrace.
In the warmth, the world feels bold,
Serenity, a tender grace.

Amidst the storm, a calm we find,
Every raindrop, love's caress.
With each step, our souls unwind,
Carried forth in quiet bless.

Through the mist, we see anew,
Colors blooming, pure delight.
Drenched in dreams, we push on through,
Lasting echoes fill the night.

As we wander, peace will stay,
Guiding us on this soaked path.
In the rain, we lose our way,
But find joy in nature's wrath.

Grains of Truth Beneath Leafy Canopies

In whispered winds the secrets sway,
Beneath the leaves where shadows play.
Truths like grains in soil reside,
Awaiting sun to guide their stride.

Softly spoken tales of old,
In every rustling leaf unfold.
Nature's voice, a gentle hum,
In leafy depths, the wisdom comes.

Through tangled roots, a story weaves,
Of time and growth, of hope and leaves.
The canopy a watchful eye,
Where truths revealed in silence lie.

A dance of light through branches made,
Each flicker shows the paths we've laid.
Grains of truth beneath the green,
In nature's heart, where all is seen.

So pause a while, breathe deep the air,
In leafy canopies, we share.
And know the truth, though seldom spoken,
In quiet woods, our hearts are open.

Tales Inscribed in Rain's Silence

When raindrops fall on thirsty ground,
They tell of stories lost, yet found.
In silence deep, each droplet sings,
Of fleeting dreams and whispered things.

The earth absorbs each tale anew,
In glistening beads the past breaks through.
Remembered faces, long since gone,
Awakened in the rain's soft song.

Clouds gather round like old friends near,
To share their lore, to dry each tear.
Every storm a page turned bright,
In nature's book of dark and light.

With every splash, we learn to see,
The beauty found in memory.
Tales inscribed with each gentle fall,
In rain's silence, we hear it all.

So let it rain, let stories flow,
In silent drops, our spirits grow.
From sorrow brewed to joy, we gain,
A world alive with tales of rain.

Chorus of the Teardrop Trees

In twilight's glow, the branches weep,
Their gentle tears a promise keep.
A chorus sung by leaves so bright,
In harmony with fading light.

Each teardrop holds a tale of grief,
Yet gives the heart a sense of relief.
Among the boughs, a solace found,
Where sorrow's song becomes the sound.

Through whispered winds, a prayer takes flight,
As trees embrace the fading night.
In every drop, a memory lies,
Reflections caught in darkening skies.

These trees of tears, they stand so tall,
Their beauty shines through every fall.
A testament to pain and glee,
In nature's arms, we're truly free.

So listen close to what they say,
In teardrop tones, as shadows play.
The chorus of the trees resound,
In every sigh, a world unbound.

Footprints Through the Murky Veil

In shadows deep, where secrets lie,
Footprints trace the path nearby.
Through murky veils of misty gray,
Lost tales await the light of day.

Each step a whisper, soft and slight,
Guides the heart through endless night.
With every mark upon the ground,
A story sleeps, yet waits to sound.

The fog embraces, thick and cold,
Wrapped in tales that time has told.
Yet in the gloom, a spark may gleam,
To show the way, to chase the dream.

As dawn breaks forth, the shadows fade,
Revealing truths the night had made.
Footprints lead to new horizons,
Through murky veils, the light arrives on.

So tread with care, and mind the path,
For every step can lead to wrath.
Yet in the journey, we discern,
The heart's true fire, the chance to learn.

Stories Clad in Moisture

Whispers dance in the night air,
Tales of shadows, soft and rare.
Dewdrops glisten like memories,
Each drop tells a story with ease.

Mossy carpets of emerald green,
Nature's quilt, a serene scene.
Footfalls echo on misty trails,
In this realm where silence prevails.

The brook hums a forgotten tune,
Underneath the watchful moon.
Every wave a tale retold,
In a world both tender and bold.

Clouds drift in a gentle maze,
Veils of gray in a tranquil haze.
Beneath them, life breathes and sighs,
In this land where stories rise.

Raindrops fall like whispered dreams,
Nature weaves its silver seams.
In the wet earth, secrets unfold,
Stories clad in moisture, untold.

Conversations with the Clouded Canopy

Leaves murmur in the softest breeze,
Secrets shared among the trees.
Branches stretch like open arms,
Welcoming thoughts, their gentle charms.

Sunlight filters through the green,
Casting shadows, a quiet scene.
Each gust carries a voice, sincere,
In the canopy, magic is near.

Birds chorus with vibrant glee,
Notes that climb like ancient trees.
Their melodies wound through the air,
Singing tales of joy and care.

Beneath the canopy's embrace,
Time slows down, finds its place.
Conversations of heart and soul,
In the whispers, we feel whole.

Clouds drift by, a soft parade,
Carrying dreams that never fade.
In this realm where voices blend,
Every moment, a story to send.

Lyrics of the Rain-Kissed Earth

Petrichor rises, sweet and pure,
Nature's scent, a balm, a cure.
Each droplet falls with a soft sigh,
Kissing the soil, where secrets lie.

The earth hums in vibrant hues,
Wrapped in the rhythm of morning dew.
Whispers echo through the grass,
Songs of life in harmony pass.

An orchestra of fluttering leaves,
In every moment, the heart believes.
Rain-painted skies weave tales anew,
In the tapestry of every hue.

With each storm, a memory grows,
Nature's ballad, it ebbs and flows.
Lyrics of moments in every drop,
A symphony that will never stop.

Awakening spirits in the ground,
Where melodies of life abound.
Listen close, let your heart unearth,
The songs sung by the rain-kissed earth.

The Call of Soaked Wanderings

Through misty trails, the whispers call,
Inviting dreams, both big and small.
Silvery paths that shimmer and gleam,
Guide us to the edges of a dream.

With every step, the earth sighs low,
Stories buried beneath the snow.
In puddles deep, reflections play,
Mapping journeys where spirits sway.

Drizzle dances on windows wide,
Nature's heartbeat, our faithful guide.
In the heart of storms, we find our way,
The call of soaked wanderings leads the day.

Echoes of laughter in the cool air,
Adventures waiting, truths laid bare.
Every droplet, a friend in disguise,
Holding mysteries, a world that lies.

Through the clouds, we seek the light,
Embracing shadows, surrendering fright.
For every journey, wet or dry,
The call of adventure will never die.

The Language of Fleeting Shadows

Whispers dance on twilight's breath,
As shadows twist and weave their tale.
Silhouettes that blur with the night,
In silence, secrets softly sail.

Fleeting forms that flicker and fade,
The language lost to waking eyes.
Yet in the dark, a truth conveyed,
In shadows' depth, the spirit lies.

Every flicker, a heartbeat's song,
Echoing through forgotten halls.
In their midst, we find we belong,
As dusk around us gently falls.

Embrace the whispers, let them flow,
Unravel tales that time forgot.
In fleeting shadows' tender glow,
Awake the dreams that we once sought.

With waning light, our fears take flight,
While shadows cloak the night's refrain.
In the stillness, we find our sight,
And dance with shadows once again.

Silken Threads of Silver Drizzle

Beneath the sky of softest gray,
Silken threads of drizzle fall.
Each drop a tale, a sweet ballet,
In nature's arms, we feel it all.

The whispers of the rain's caress,
As silver glimmers on the ground.
Each moment wrapped in tenderness,
In every drop, joy can be found.

The world is washed, anew, alive,
With colors bright and scents so sweet.
Within this dance, our spirits strive,
As silver threads, the earth's heartbeat.

We gather close, under the storm,
With laughter shared and stories spun.
In drizzles soft, our hearts stay warm,
As silken threads bind everyone.

And when the sun breaks through the night,
The silver fades; yet love remains.
In memories of that soft light,
We find our peace amid the rains.

Unveiled Dreams on Glen Trails

Upon the glen where daylight gleams,
Unveiled dreams begin to roam.
With every step, a whisper seems,
To call the heart back home.

A path adorned with emerald hues,
Where every leaf has tales to tell.
In nature's breath, our spirits muse,
And in her arms, we dwell.

The breeze carries a song of grace,
Echoing through the ancient pines.
In this embrace, we find our place,
As time within us intertwines.

Beneath the arch of endless skies,
With stars that wink from ages past.
We trace the tale of lullabies,
In dreams unveiled, our shadows cast.

With every step, the glen imparts,
A tapestry of life unique.
Guided by the whispers of hearts,
In trails of dreams, we seek and speak.

Threads of Nostalgia in the Mud

In puddles deep, the memories lie,
Threads of nostalgia, raw and real.
With every step, we wonder why,
These moments past, we still can feel.

Each print we leave, a story shared,
Of laughter, tears, and childhood games.
In mud-streaked paths, our hearts declared,
The joy we found, the love that claims.

The rain brings forth a playful dance,
As echoes of the past unfold.
With every splash, we take a chance,
On memories that never grow old.

Through tangled roots and winding trails,
We walk the lines of days gone by.
In muddy shoes, the heart prevails,
As threads of time weave and fly.

So let us wander, hand in hand,
Through paths where history intertwines.
In every step, let us understand,
The beauty found in life's designs.

Conversations with Clouded Canopies

Whispers travel in the air,
Murmurs through the tangled leaves,
Secrets linger everywhere,
In twilight's soft, embracing eves.

Shadows dance, a fleeting show,
Above where dreams and silence meet,
Echoes of the winds that blow,
In rhythm slow, their gentle beat.

Through canopies, the echoes flow,
Where light mingles with the shade,
Stories only branches know,
In this enchanted, fleeting glade.

Clouds drift softly, touch the trees,
Caressing bark with tender sighs,
Nature hums in melodies,
As dusk unfurls its violet skies.

Beneath the boughs, the world unwinds,
In quietude, reflections glide,
The heart of nature unconfines,
In sacred whispers, dreams abide.

Harmonics of Hushed Waters

Ripples glide on silver streams,
Silent songs of ancient lands,
Flowing softly like our dreams,
Carved by time and gentle hands.

Beneath the surface, life does weave,
A symphony of heart and flow,
In every wave, a tale to grieve,
Yet also joy, as rivers grow.

Stone and current smooth the way,
Each journey finds a home to dwell,
In stillness, beauty finds its sway,
With every sound, a whispered spell.

The twilight hum, a serenade,
Over pebbled beds it glides,
In every note, a truth displayed,
Where nature's timeless song abides.

Hushed waters speak in tranquil tones,
To every ear who stops to hear,
In liquid hymns, the heart atones,
With harmonics drawing near.

The Sigh of Saturated Soil

After the rain, a fragrance dwells,
Earth awakens, fresh and alive,
Soft whispers rise from hidden wells,
Where life receives its chance to thrive.

Roots embrace with eager crawl,
As droplets cradle every seed,
In silken soil, a silent call,
Where hope emerges from each deed.

A sigh escapes, a fervent plea,
From depths where dreams and wishes grow,
In every grain, a symphony,
Of stories waiting just to show.

Raindrops dance on surfaces wide,
The earth takes breath with every fall,
In harmony, nature's pride,
Pulses through the roots of all.

The sigh it carries, soft yet strong,
Beneath the weight of verdant grace,
In soil's embrace, we all belong,
A sacred bond, a nurturing space.

Beneath the Weeping Elm

Beneath the elm, where shadows play,
Branches bow with whispers low,
In gentle arcs, they sway and sway,
To secrets only they might know.

Leaves tremble with the evening's breath,
Surroundings hush as twilight calls,
In silence, ponder life and death,
As twilight's curtain softly falls.

The air is thick with stories spun,
Of lovers past and time's embrace,
In each soft rustle, tales begun,
Underneath the elm's warm grace.

Here, moments linger, dreams entreat,
With nature's choir, a timeless sound,
In shade, our hearts find solace sweet,
Amongst the roots that weave the ground.

So come and sit, let thoughts unfurl,
Under the branches, sky's great dome,
In this embrace, let worries swirl,
Beneath the elm, we find our home.

Murmured Secrets on a Moist Journey

Beneath the greening boughs, whispers swell,
Promises tucked in shadows where they dwell.
Dripping leaves tell tales of the night,
Murmured secrets lost in dawn's light.

Each step on the path, a soft refrain,
Echoes of journeys traced through the rain.
Footsteps dance on puddles, liquid glass,
A world reborn, vibrant memories pass.

In the mist, dreams linger, softly spun,
Voices of nature, whispers begun.
Clouds drift lazily, cradles of gray,
In this moist embrace, we wander and sway.

The map in my heart marks every stream,
Tracing the edges of each fleeting dream.
Where waters converge, we find our way,
Murmured secrets on this moist ballet.

So let the journey unfold, slow yet true,
With every breath, the cosmos anew.
In a world where nature's pulse aligns,
Murmured secrets echo in the pines.

Raindrop Revelations on Lonely Paths

On lonely paths where raindrops play,
Silence hangs soft, as night turns to day.
Each drop a tale that the earth unfolds,
Revelations born, in whispering folds.

Clouds gather round, a shroud of thought,
Every trickle speaks of battles fought.
Feel the rhythm of the falling sound,
In the solitude, true solace found.

The air, it sparkles with secrets untold,
Raindrop revelations, shimmering gold.
Memories linger on the tips of leaves,
In the quiet moments, the heart believes.

Footsteps echo on this timeless road,
Carrying dreams, a weightless load.
Through the drizzles, I wander and roam,
Raindrop revelations guide me home.

The sky weeps softly, a gentle embrace,
In each droplet, I find my place.
Through lonely paths where shadows align,
Raindrop revelations, a love divine.

The Intersection of Sky and Soil

Where the sky kisses the earth, a blend,
Blues and browns weave, horizons extend.
Mountains rise high, reaching for grace,
The intersection of space, time, and place.

Each breath drawn in, a fusion of life,
Nature's cadence softens the strife.
Grains of soil cradle stories beneath,
In the dance of elements, a quiet wreath.

Beneath the wide arch of the endless blue,
Every flower's blush tells of secrets anew.
Clouds drift lazily, their shadows dart,
Painting the canvas of a breathing heart.

In this realm where opposites meet,
Harmony lingers, bittersweet.
Roots dig deep, reaching for the sky,
The intersection of existences sigh.

Through seasons' embrace, we learn and grow,
In the pulse of nature, our spirits flow.
Between earth and heavens, we find our goal,
The intersection of sky and soil.

In the twilight's glow, everything aligns,
A tapestry woven from nature's designs.
Here we stand, in awe and in toil,
At the intersection of sky and soil.

Silent Conversations with the Storm

In the hush before the tempest brews,
A silence lingers, wrapped in hues.
Clouds converge in ominous grace,
Silent conversations in nature's embrace.

The wind carries whispers, secrets untold,
Stories of journeys through torrents bold.
In shadows that dance, a rhythm is born,
Silent conversations, the world reborn.

Raindrops tap softly, a delicate song,
Each one a heartbeat where we belong.
Nature listens, in stillness it waits,
For the thunder's roar, as fate narrates.

Lightning traces lines across the night,
An artist's brush, a flash of light.
In the chaos, a strange harmony,
Silent conversations with infinity.

As storms pass, calmness finds its way,
In the aftermath, the heart learns to sway.
A dialogue with nature's pulse resounds,
Silent conversations, where wisdom abounds.

Embrace the storm, let it unfurl,
For in every tempest, a truth will swirl.
In the stillness that follows, we may find,
Silent conversations with the divine.

Patterns in the Waterlogged Ground

Mud ripples stretch and sway,
Tracing tales of yesterday,
Footprints fade, then reappear,
Echoes linger, soft and clear.

A dance of shadows on the clay,
Nature's brush in wild array,
Colors merge, then slip away,
In the dusk, they softly play.

Hues of earth, a tapestry,
Beneath the leaves, a mystery,
Whispers in the gentle rain,
Marking paths like hidden stain.

Life entwines in soft embrace,
In the ground, we find our place,
Water sings a secret song,
In this realm, we all belong.

Footfalls echo far and wide,
In the mud, the dreams reside,
Patterns weave their silent art,
Crafting stories, each a part.

Whispers from the Stony Path

Pebbles speak in muted tones,
Rustling leaves and shifting stones,
Secrets hid in cracks and crevices,
Nature's breath, the mind's premises.

Worn by time, the earth stands tall,
Carrying tales of rise and fall,
Every step a fleeting trace,
A journey through this ancient space.

Mossy blankets on rugged slopes,
Crowning dreams and buried hopes,
Thorns and blooms entwined as one,
Navigating 'neath the sun.

Thoughts unspoken as we roam,
This winding path, a second home,
Each stone holds a tale to tell,
In whispers where the shadows dwell.

Footprints mark the time we spend,
On this road that seems to bend,
With each pause, the heart feels free,
In the stillness, we just be.

Nocturnal Secrets and Stormy Trails

Night unfolds her velvet shroud,
Silence wraps the world so loud,
In shadows deep, the secrets hide,
Where stormy breezes dare to glide.

Stars emerge with whispered sighs,
Dreams take flight in moonlit skies,
Thunder rumbles in the deep,
While the restless forest sleeps.

Footsteps echo on the ground,
As the nightingale resounds,
Every sigh a breath of fate,
Escaping through the iron gate.

Lightning paints the sky with grace,
Tracing whispers on my face,
In this tempest, find the light,
Illuminating shadows bright.

Nocturnal tales of undying flame,
In stormy trails, we trace the name,
Of those who walked the paths of night,
Chasing shadows into light.

Reflections in the Raindrop's Dance

Glistening jewels on the leaf,
Each drop a story, beyond belief,
Swaying gently in the breeze,
Nature's pulse, a soft reprise.

Mirrored skies in puddles deep,
Holding rapture, secrets keep,
Dancing rhythms on the ground,
Singing soft, a tranquil sound.

Colors blur in liquid grace,
As raindrops trace their silken race,
Momentum lost, yet time stands still,
In this moment, we all feel.

Sunlight breaks as shadows part,
Painting hope within the heart,
In reflections, we see our past,
In raindrop's dance, our dreams are cast.

Each gentle fall tells us to pause,
Celebrate the world because,
In every drop, a life unfolds,
A tale of warmth in the cold.

Beneath the Canopy: Nature's Confessions

Whispers float on gentle breeze,
The canopy sways with ease.
Secrets hide in every shade,
Nature's truths, softly laid.

Sunlight weaves through emerald lace,
Creatures flutter, find their space.
Roots entwined, a silent vow,
Life persists, here and now.

Mossy carpets, whispers low,
Echoes of the streams that flow.
Birds in chorus, songs retold,
Nature's confessions, brave and bold.

Leaves converse, a rustling sound,
In this haven, peace is found.
Beneath the boughs, hearts will mend,
In this realm, we transcend.

Each moment held, a precious gem,
Beneath the trees, we lose the stem.
Laughing streams and sighing leaves,
Nature's breath, our soul receives.

Shadows Danced by Rain's Embrace

Pattering drops on thirsty ground,
Whispers rise, a rhythmic sound.
Shadows twirl in puddle's gleam,
Nature's ballet, a fleeting dream.

Murky skies with silver light,
Clouds amassed, a cloaked delight.
Dancing vines in sudden flow,
Harmony, in rain's soft show.

Graceful moves, a playful sway,
Shadows frolic, drift away.
The world awash in muted hues,
Rain recalls forgotten views.

Through the droplets, colors spark,
Hidden joy found in the dark.
Each splash echoes, memories chase,
A rhythm born in the rain's embrace.

With every sigh, a tale unfolds,
In the dance, the heart beholds.
Rain's soft music, all around,
In each shadow, peace is found.

A Soliloquy of the Soggy World

In the quiet, raindrops speak,
A symphony of the meek.
Puddles gather, tales to tell,
In this soggy, silent swell.

Muffled echoes, streets reflect,
Nature's sigh, we can't neglect.
Each moment drips with meaning clear,
In the downpour, we draw near.

Mist hangs low like a gentle veil,
A soft touch, a whispered trail.
Every drop a story spun,
Under clouds, we come undone.

Through blurred views, the world shifts shades,
Soggy paths where silence pervades.
A soliloquy of earth and sky,
In this drumming, secrets lie.

We find solace in the rain,
In the whispers, healing pain.
A soggy world, a tender balm,
Wrapped in droplets, soft and calm.

The Elegy of Fallen Leaves

Once adorned in vibrant hues,
Now they dance in autumn's muse.
Leaves cascade, a gentle flight,
Whispers of their final sight.

Crimson, gold, in breezes twirl,
Memories in each spiral swirl.
The ground, a tapestry of grace,
An elegy for nature's face.

Bare branches reach for clouded skies,
Underneath, their beauty lies.
Nature mourns in soft embrace,
Time to rest, to find their place.

In the quiet, whispers wane,
Leaves will lie, but not in vain.
Each leaf tells a story brief,
In their fall, a fleeting grief.

A tapestry of life once lived,
Lessons in the leaves they've given.
The elegy, a sweet farewell,
In every leaf, a tale to tell.

Glimmers of Light in Hidden Places

In shadows deep, soft beams do play,
A flicker bright at close of day.
Through tangled roots and leaves of green,
A secret world waits to be seen.

Each spark a hope that guides the way,
In corners where the timid stay.
It dances lightly, secretive,
A grace within the dark to live.

And as the dusk begins to creep,
These tiny lights, they gently leap.
With every glint, a promise blooms,
Illuminating hidden rooms.

Not just the bold or strong may find,
These glimmers sweet that soothe the mind.
In quiet moments, they remain,
A whisper soft amidst the pain.

So pause and look, for there they lie,
In every nook, beneath the sky.
Embrace the light that softly glows,
In hidden places, beauty grows.

The Interlude of Raindrop Reflections

As raindrops fall, the world takes pause,
A symphony without applause.
Each drop a note, each splash a sigh,
Beneath the gray, the dreams will fly.

In puddles formed on cobblestone,
Reflections dance, as if they've grown.
Mirrored skies with clouds so near,
In every drop, a whispered tear.

The air is sweet, the earth drinks deep,
While nature weaves its secrets, steep.
With every thrum, the heart expands,
In this soft rain, love understands.

As sunlight peeks through silver strands,
The world transforms by gentle hands.
And in this moment, life anew,
Each heartbeat sings, each thought rings true.

Even in storms, we find a way,
To cherish light amidst the gray.
In every droplet, joy reflects,
In nature's pause, we find   .

Whispers Through the Thunder's Veil

In stormy nights, the thunder speaks,
A booming voice that gently peaks.
Yet in the noise, soft whispers wane,
Carried on winds, a sweet refrain.

Through veils of gray, the shadows creep,
While hidden truths stir in their sleep.
Each flash of light, a fleeting breath,
A dance of life, a dance with death.

In quiet moments, hearts ignite,
With whispered dreams that take to flight.
Beneath the roar, they find their way,
In thunder's grasp, the night will sway.

So listen close, for joy is near,
In every gust, a song to hear.
Embrace the clash, the wild, the bold,
For whispers weave the tales retold.

And when the storm at last will pass,
The echoes linger, shadows cast.
For in the chaos, truths unveil,
A symphony through thunder's veil.

Memories Inked by Wet Leaves

Upon the ground, the leaves are wet,
With every drop, the past is met.
In colors bright, they tell a tale,
Of golden hours and whispers pale.

Each leaf a page so richly scribed,
Of laughter shared, of love imbibed.
And as the rain does softly fall,
These moments linger, memory's call.

With every step, a rustle found,
While echoes of the past abound.
In nature's book, the stories blend,
A chapter lived, a time to mend.

The ink of life, it stains the ground,
In every hue, lost dreams are found.
And as we tread on paths unseen,
We dance with ghosts of what has been.

So let the rain renew the sheet,
With wet leaves underfoot, we meet.
For every drop that splashes free,
Is just a part of you and me.

Where Soft Drizzles Play

Gentle drops from skies descend,
Whispering secrets to leaves and bend.
Each petal glistens, kissed by grace,
In the quiet, a soft embrace.

Paths of gravel, damp and bright,
Shadows dance in soft twilight.
Nature's symphony, pure and clear,
In this moment, I feel no fear.

Above, the clouds begin to swirl,
While laughter of the rain unfurl.
A lullaby, sweet, and divine,
Kissing earth, a sacred sign.

Footsteps muffled, heartbeats slow,
Tender memories start to grow.
With each splash, a spirit free,
Where soft drizzles play, a glee.

In circles drawn, reflections gleam,
Beneath the surface, I dare dream.
Held in arms of nature's song,
In this haven, I belong.

Edges of Twilight's Tender Tears

Where day meets night, the colors blend,
A whispering breeze, a gentle friend.
The sky, a canvas, paints anew,
Each shade of hope, a soft debut.

Dusk wraps around like a silken shawl,
As shadows lengthen, they gently call.
Stars begin to twinkle, bold and bright,
In the edges of this fading light.

With every heartbeat, time will flow,
Memories linger, ebb, and glow.
The tears of twilight softly fall,
A gentle sigh, a lasting thrall.

From horizons wide, dreams take flight,
In tender tears of the night.
Voices whisper, secrets shared,
In twilight's arms, souls laid bare.

As darkness wraps the world in peace,
The echoes of the day will cease.
In every heartbeat, love will rise,
Edge of twilight, where magic lies.

Reflections in Woven Waterways

Beneath the surface, ripples flow,
Carrying stories only they know.
Mirrored skies in liquid art,
Each moment captured, a beating heart.

Banks adorned with flowers bright,
Veils of green in soft daylight.
Quiet whispers, gently sway,
In woven pathways where dreams play.

The dance of fish, a fleeting gleam,
In currents swift, they weave a dream.
Sunlight dapples on the stream,
Nature's breath, a sacred theme.

In every ripple, a tale unfolds,
Of longing deep and mysteries told.
Together we join, heart and soul,
Reflections in waterways, we are whole.

When night descends, the stars align,
Their shimmering light, a sacred sign.
In tranquil waters, fears away,
We find our peace, where dreams stay.

Quintessence of Dampened Footsteps

Along the path where shadows creep,
The quiet murmurs, the earth will weep.
Each step a echo, soft and low,
In this realm where moments flow.

Puddles form with every rain,
Little worlds where dreams remain.
The rhythm of my heart aligns,
With every tread, sweet peace entwines.

Whispers of the past resound,
In the hush where lost can be found.
Nature's breath in cool embrace,
In dampened footsteps, I find my place.

As twilight wanes, the stars appear,
Each tiny spark, a wish sincere.
With every step that I reclaim,
The essence of my truth, aflame.

In this quiet, I am free,
The world unfolds its mystery.
In dampened footsteps, life unfolds,
Quintessence of the heart, retold.

The Narrative of a Stormy Path

In shadows deep, the thunder rolls,
Each step we take, the darkness trolls.
Yet through the clouds, a glimmer shines,
Our hearts persist, in twisted lines.

With every gust that pulls us near,
We face the fears, embrace the sheer.
The soil beneath, it cracks and breaks,
Yet onward still, our spirit wakes.

Through tempest's rage, we carve our way,
The storm will pass; it won't betray.
And in the end, a tale we tell,
Of how we faced the storm so well.

The path is wild, the journey long,
But in our souls, we find a song.
Resilience flows, a river fierce,
The storm may shake, but we'll not pierce.

So let the winds, and rain, collide,
We walk, we run, with hope as guide.
For every storm that comes our way,
We'll stand as one, come what may.

Dripping With Hope and Silence

A raindrop falls on quiet ground,
In whispered tones, the silence found.
Each drop a promise yet to bloom,
In stillness lies the heart's own room.

The earth drinks deep, a parched embrace,
As hope unfurls in nature's grace.
With every pulse, the world awakes,
The sound of life, as stillness breaks.

In gentle sways, the branches hum,
A lullaby where dreams become.
With every sigh, the shadows lift,
In drizzled light, we find the gift.

So let the rain's soft fingers trace,
The edges of our cosmic space.
For dripping hope, it dances free,
In silken threads of harmony.

Through quiet storms, we learn to trust,
That life can flourish, roots in dust.
As silence fills the air around,
We breathe in peace, our hearts unbound.

Voices Surrendered to the Storm

The wind it howls, a haunting song,
Calling forth the brave and strong.
With hearts laid bare, we hear the call,
Together we rise, we will not fall.

In tempest's grip, we find our ground,
Bound by the song that we have found.
Voices merge with thunder's might,
A symphony born from the night.

Each drop that falls, a tale unfolds,
Of hopes and fears that we behold.
In every clash, in every roar,
The heart beats loud, we seek for more.

With arms spread wide, we face the gale,
A chorus strong, we will not pale.
Embracing all the storm can bring,
Our voices rise; we learn to sing.

Through raging skies, we find our way,
In every storm, we choose to stay.
For in the chaos, hearts align,
Voices strong as stars that shine.

Let winds collide with spirits free,
In harmony, we dare to be.
Surrendered to the storm's embrace,
We'll find our peace; we'll find our place.

Softly Spoken Winds on Wet Trails

A whisper rides the morning air,
Soft winds that weave with gentle care.
Through trails of dew, our footsteps glide,
With nature's grace and hearts opened wide.

Each step a dance, a fleeting sigh,
The world around begins to fly.
In every rustle, a secret shared,
The softest winds, in silence bared.

Through misty paths, we wander free,
Embracing all that's yet to be.
As sunlight breaks, the shadows fade,
In every breeze, our hopes parade.

With whispered tales, the trees confess,
The winds bestow their soft caress.
Each rustling leaf, a softer song,
In nature's arms, we all belong.

So let the trails, both wet and wild,
Lead us forth, in wonder's child.
With softly spoken winds as guide,
We walk as one, through heart and stride.

The journey calls, our spirits soar,
In every breath, we live, explore.
For in the winds, a truth we find,
Together forged, forever aligned.

www.ingramcontent.com/pod-product-compliance
Lightning Source LLC
Chambersburg PA
CBHW060419160125
20422CB00001B/331